Architectural Details
Spain and the Mediterranean

S. F. "Jerry" Cook III & Tina Skinner

4880 Lower Valley Road, Atglen, PA 19310 USA

Copyright © 2005 by S.F. "Jerry" Cook III &
Schiffer Publishing, Ltd.
Library of Congress Control Number: 2005925752

All rights reserved. No part of this work may be reproduced or used in any form or by any means—graphic, electronic, or mechanical, including photocopying or information storage and retrieval systems—without written permission from the publisher.
The scanning, uploading and distribution of this book or any part thereof via the Internet or via any other means without the permission of the publisher is illegal and punishable by law. Please purchase only authorized editions and do not participate in or encourage the electronic piracy of copyrighted materials.
"Schiffer," "Schiffer Publishing Ltd. & Design," and the "Design of pen and ink well" are registered trademarks of Schiffer Publishing Ltd.

Designed by "Sue"
Type set in AlgerianD/Dutch801 Rm BT

ISBN: 0-7643-2307-5
Printed in China

Published by Schiffer Publishing Ltd.
4880 Lower Valley Road
Atglen, PA 19310
Phone: (610) 593-1777; Fax: (610) 593-2002
E-mail: Info@schifferbooks.com

For the largest selection of fine reference books on this and related subjects, please visit our web site at
www.schifferbooks.com
We are always looking for people to write books on new and related subjects. If you have an idea for a book please contact us at the above address.

This book may be purchased from the publisher.
Include $3.95 for shipping.
Please try your bookstore first.
You may write for a free catalog.

In Europe, Schiffer books are distributed by
Bushwood Books
6 Marksbury Ave.
Kew Gardens
Surrey TW9 4JF England
Phone: 44 (0) 20 8392-8585; Fax: 44 (0) 20 8392-9876
E-mail: info@bushwoodbooks.co.uk
Free postage in the U.K., Europe; air mail at cost.

Contents

Foreword 4
Introduction 5
Houses – Country Type 6
Buildings – City Type 17
Street Scenes 29
Street Façades and Entrances 40
Doorways 51
Door Details – Grilles – Gates 63
Balconies 75
Window Grilles and Shutters 86
Roofs – Towers – Cornices 98
Courts and Patios 110
Garden Details 120
Miscellaneous 132
Bibliography 144

Foreword

There is perhaps no section of greater interest to Californians than Spain and the countries bordering the western Mediterranean.

This is due to the fact that the greater portion of southwestern America was discovered and settled by adventurers and missionaries from southern Spain. The picturesque old missions and other interesting structures built by them along the Pacific slopes, and evidencing their endeavors, devotion, and struggles, are reminiscent of the beautiful buildings of their homeland.

Then, the climate, topography, and other natural conditions found in southern Europe and northern Africa are strikingly similar to conditions found in the southwest section of our own country. Indeed, in traveling along the Mediterranean littoral, one is constantly reminded of Southern California; the same general aspect of the landscape; the same character of wild growth, the same soft colorings, and the same balmy, congenial atmosphere. The roadways are frequently bordered with eucalyptus and palms; the hillsides are dotted with citrus orchards, olive groves, and vineyards; and the parks, plazas, and patios are filled with the same trees, shrubs, vines, and flowering plants, growing in the same luxuriance and profusion as in Southern California.

But undoubtedly the main reason for the rapidly increasing interest in the western Mediterranean countries is the growing appreciation of the fact that the logical, fitting, and altogether appropriate architecture for California and the Pacific Southwest is a style inspired and suggested by the architecture of those countries.

The fundamental characteristics of the architecture of all the western Mediterranean countries are substantially the same.

The walls of the buildings were built of rough masonry finished on the exterior with stucco, whitewashed or tinted in light pastel shades harmonizing with the landscape.

The roofs were constructed either flat or low-pitched, covered with red, burned clay tiles.

Ornament was used with great restraint or discrimination, and not without definite reason and purpose. It usually consisted of simple, well-designed mouldings, corbels, brackets, pilasters and columns, concentrated and disposed so as to leave generous areas of plain wall surfaces.

Exterior interest, attractiveness, and charm was obtained by wrought iron, wood, or stuccoed window grilles, shutters, balconies, or other similar practical features.

The focal point of the exterior design was usually the main entrance, the doors of which were sometimes elaborately paneled and ornamented with wrought iron hardware, studs, and bolt heads of beautiful pattern.

Courts, patios, and gardens were quite an indispensable feature of the architectural treatment. These were made intimate with the buildings by means of colonnades, arcades, loggias and paved terraces. The garden areas were made inviting and gay with fountains, pools, pergolas, polychrome tile seats, exedras, and other interesting garden accessories. Flowering plants in terra cotta pots were also used profusely in the gardens, on the parapets and covering the balconies.

Through centuries of development, the foregoing basic features have been found most essential and harmonious in the design of buildings for an environment such as exists in California; therefore, it is reasonable to presume they are the fundamental characteristics of the logical architectural style for the Pacific southwest.

The author endeavored, in a recent trip through the Mediterranean countries, to photograph such details of their buildings and gardens as could be appropriately used, or at least serve as inspiration, for developing the California style.

From some six hundred negatives made in southern Europe, north Africa, and the island of the Mediterranean, such details were selected for this work as would be of the greatest interest and value to California architects, and these have been classified and arranged to facilitate their use in the drafting room.

RICHARD REQUA
San Diego, California
September 30th, 1926

Introduction

Richard Requa earned himself wide regard as an architect pioneering the "southern California" style of architecture during the 1920s and '30s. With a missionary zeal, he set out to preserve existing Spanish Colonial architecture, and to spread an appreciation of "authentic" Mediterranean style throughout his profession.

Requa was born in Illinois in 1881, and moved to Norfolk, Nebraska with his family. He studied electrical engineering at Norfolk College before following his family to San Diego in 1900. His architectural apprenticeship began in the office of Irving J. Gill, an accredited architect. Married to Viola Hust in 1908, Requa left Gill in 1912 to join in partnership with Frank L. Mead.

Mead & Requa together pursued the historical heritage of the Colonial style of Old Mexico, the Pueblos of the Southwest, and the Moorish features from Spain and North Africa. Together they designed the business section of the southern California community of Ojai, including the post office, a Catholic church, a hotel, and many private residences.

In 1920, Mead left the firm, and Herbert L. Jackson, a structural engineer, joined to form Requa & Jackson. Theirs became the most sought-after firm for the booming 1920s, and their Southern California Architecture dominated the San Diego scene.

Requa was also fortunate in landing the patronage of Coy Burnett, president of the Monolith Portland Cement Company in Colorado. Besides designing Burnett's home, Requa also earned two extensive European trips paid for by Monolith during which he traveled throughout the Mediterranean region photographing the native architecture. He culled his images to produce two pioneering works. The one reprinted here, *Architectural Details, Spain and the Mediterranean*, was published first as a loose folio of 1,000 copies, and later in a bound edition of 500 copies in 1926. His next study, *Old World Inspiration for American Architecture* (1929) was published as a bound volume only and also supplied to libraries and architects courtesy of Monolith. In 1928, he exhibited his photography in the Fine Arts Gallery of Balboa Park in San Diego, and earned high reviews from area newspapers.

In a 1937 book, *Inside Lights on the Building of San Diego's Exposition, 1935*, he recounted the work of preserving and further developing the 1915 Exposition Buildings. Requa engineered repairs in order to save the building that went on to become the landmark of Balboa Park. The Exposition drew over seven million visitors, and helped revive a flagging local economy. More importantly, perhaps, Requa managed to seed those visitors and countless visitors and residents with, as he wrote, a desire "for greater harmony in their own lives and surroundings."

Requa's career was cut short when he died of a heart attack in 1941 while working in his office. However, his legacy is huge. His "Southern California Style" imprint – white stucco, heavily tiled roofs, wrought iron ornamentation, unique chimney designs, Moorish arches, and polychrome tile fountains and accents – remains on many homes, including two of his own, in the San Diego area. He also left his mark in the form of the Del Mar Castle, the County Administration Center on Pacific Highway, the Torrey Pines State Park visitors center (originally a restaurant on the road from Los Angeles to San Diego), Pine Hills Lodge in Julian, the Mount Helix Open Air Theater, the Casa de Pico Motel in Old Town that became the Bazaar del Mundo, now the anchor of Old Town State Historic Park. He was commissioned by the Santa Fe Land Company to lay out the commercial district and many of the first homes for Rancho Santa Fe.

The images that inspired Requa and his colleagues sol long ago have not lost their power. As interest once again revives with regard to Spanish Colonial architecture, Requa's work reemerges as an invaluable aid to the limitless imagination of architects and designers.

Houses – Country Type

A hillside farmhouse overlooking Funchal, Madeira.

Houses - Country Style 7

A TYPICAL RURAL COTTAGE OF ANDALUSIA.

A ROADSIDE COTTAGE NEAR ALGECIRAS, SOUTHERN SPAIN.

CHARACTERISTIC TREATMENT OF COUNTRY HOUSES IN SOUTHERN SPAIN.

10 Houses - Country Style

A road overseer's cottage, Province of Cadiz.

A ROADHOUSE ON THE HIGHWAY SKIRTING THE BAY OF ALGECIRAS.

12   Houses - Country Style

A roadside cottage near San Roque, southern Spain.

THE SMALL FARMHOUSES OF SOUTHERN SPAIN, ETC.

14 Houses - Country Style

A COUNTRY HOUSE IN THE SUBURBS OF GRANADA, SPAIN.

Houses - Country Style 15

A TYPICAL RANCH IN SOUTHERN SPAIN.

16   Houses - Country Style

A cottage on the road to Tarifa, southern Spain.

Buildings – City Type

Street façade of the Oriental Hotel, Algiers.

18 Buildings – City Type

LATE EXAMPLE OF MOORISH ARCHITECTURE, ALGIERS.

A BUILDING IN GIBRALTAR.

20 Buildings – City Type

HOUSES IN THE CATHEDRAL SQUARE, ALGECIRAS.

Buildings – City Type 21

A TYPICAL HOUSE IN RONDA.

22 Buildings – City Type

A LIQUOR SHOP IN SEVILLE.

A BUILDING WITH AN INTERESTING CORNICE, GRANADA.

24 Buildings – City Type

AN OLD BUILDING IN CORDOVA.

SALES ROOM OF A TILE FACTORY IN TOLEDO.

26 Buildings – City Type

Modern residential architecture in Sitges.

Modern buildings along the ocean boulevard, Sitges.

28 Buildings – City Type

ANOTHER MODERN HOME IN SITGES.

A street in Old Town, Algiers.

AN ORIENTAL STREET SCENE, TUNIS.

A STREET FACING THE SEA IN SYRACUSE, AND A STREET LEADING TO THE CATHEDRAL, CAGLIARI.

ARCHITECTURAL TREATMENT OF STREET HOUSES IN VALLETTA.

Buildings facing the main street in Marina Grande, Capri.

34   Street Scenes

A street scene in Athens, and in the city built on the steep side of a rock, Gibraltar.

A BUILDING IN ALAMEDA, CADIZ, AND A TYPICAL STREET IN CADIZ.

A STREET SCENE IN SEVILLE.

LEFT: AN OLD STREET OF THE MOORS AND TOWERS OF THE ALCAZAR, SEVILLE. RIGHT: BUILDINGS OF GRANADA VIEWED THROUGH THE OLD CITY WALL.

BUILDINGS OF GRANADA VIEWED FROM THE ENTRANCE TO THE GENERALIFE.

INTERESTING BUILDINGS IN AN OLD STREET IN CORDOVA.

Street Façades and Entrances

A house in Tunis.

A CHARACTERISTIC RESIDENTIAL STREET IN SYRACUSE.

42 Street Façades and Entrances

AN INTERESTING DOORWAY IN SYRACUSE, AND A HOODED ENTRANCE IN TOLEDO.

Street Façades of two houses in Ronda.

44   Street Façades and Entrances

DETAILS OF TWO ENTRANCES TO HOUSES IN RONDA.

ENTRANCE TO A HOUSE IN GRANADA.

46 Street Façades and Entrances

IN THE MEDIEVAL CITY OF IMPOSING ENTRANCES, SEGOVIA.

TWO ENTRANCES TO HOUSES IN SEGOVIA.

48 Street Façades and Entrances

TWO MORE CHARMING ENTRANCES IN SEGOVIA.

An old house in Barcelona.

ENTRANCE TO AN OLD COUNTRY HOUSE NEAR BARCELONA

DOORWAYS

A BEAUTIFUL ORIENTAL DOOR TREATMENT, ALGIERS.

52 Doorways

AN OLD NAIL STUDDED DOOR IN TUNIS.

MOORISH DOORWAY IN BEY'S PALACE, TUNIS.

AN INTERESTING NAIL STUDDED DOOR IN SEVILLE.

DOORWAY TO A CHURCH IN SEVILLE.

56 Doorways

Two beautiful doors in the municipal building, Barcelona.

DOORWAY TO AN OLD PALACE IN TOLEDO.

DOORWAY IN A RESTORED PALACE IN SITGES.

DOORWAY TO A MUSEUM IN SITGES.

60 Doorways

CHARACTERISTIC TREATMENT OF ENTRANCE DOORS IN TOLDEO
AND ONE OF THE MANY INTERESTING DOORS IN SITGES.

Doorways 61

NOVEL PANELING ON DOORS IN SITGES.

62   Doorways

TWO MORE VERY EFFECTIVE DOORS IN SITGES.

Door Details – Grilles – Gates

Knocker on an old Moorish door, Tunis.

64 Door Details – Grilles – Gates

A GARDEN GATE, ISLAND OF CAPRI.

ENTRANCE TO THE CATHEDRAL, SYRACUSE.

AN INTERESTING HOOD OVER AN ENTRANCE DOOR, RONDA.

Door Details – Grilles – Gates 67

DOOR TO A CHURCH IN GRANADA.

DETAIL OF SPINDLES IN A GATE, GRANADA.

Door Details – Grilles – Gates 69

AN ELABORATELY CARVED DOOR IN THE ALHAMBRA.

70 Door Details – Grilles – Gates

A SPINDLE GATE ENTRANCE TO A PATIO IN CORDOVA.

DOORKNOCKERS ON A PRIVATE HOUSE IN SEGOVIA.

ENTRANCE TO CATHEDRAL, BARCELONA.

Door Details – Grilles – Gates 73

DETAIL OF A DOOR IN SITGES.

74 Door Details – Grilles – Gates

AN ELABORATE ENTRANCE DOOR TREATMENT, SITGES.

BALCONIES

A BALCONY, ORIENTAL HOTEL, ALGECIRAS.

IN AN OLD COURTYARD, SYRACUSE

PICTURESQUE STAIRWAYS AND BALCONIES IN SYRACUSE.

BALCONIES IN ATHENS.

STAIRWAYS AND BALCONIES, ISLAND OF CAPRI.

A GARDEN ENTRANCE AND OVERHANGING BALCONIES, CAPRI, AND AN
EXAMPLE OF INTERESTING BALCONIES IN ALGECIRAS.

IN THE CITY OF BEAUTIFUL WROUGHT IRONWORK, ALGECIRAS.

HOUSE IN ALGECIRAS AND A BEAUTIFUL BALCONY IN SITGES.

A DELIGHTFUL CORNER OF A COURTYARD IN CORDOVA.

WROUGHT IRON BALCONIES, CORDOVA, AND AN INTERESTING
WROUGHT IRON BALCONY IN SITGES.

AN IRON RAILED GALLERY IN A COURTYARD, BARCELONA.

Window Grilles and Shutters

Window grilles on the Oriental Hotel, Algiers.

MOORISH TREATMENT OF A WINDOW, ALGIERS.

A HAREM TYPE WINDOW GRILLE, TUNIS.

A CHARACTERISTIC WIDOW GRILLE IN ALGECIRAS.

DECORATIVE TREATMENT OF A WINDOW IN A TOWER,
CORDOVA, AND A WINDOW GRILLE IN RONDA.

WROUGHT IRONWORK ON A BUILDING IN SEVILLE.

92 Window Grilles and Shutters

Rose windows in a church, Seville.

MOORISH SHUTTERS, WINDOW IN A CHAPEL, BARCELONA, AND
INTERESTING PANELED SHUTTERS TO A HOUSE, GRANADA.

94 Window Grilles and Shutters

An unusual wrought iron window grille in Ronda and an elaborate window grille in Sitges.

MOORISH DECORATION, ENTRANCE TO THE MOSQUE, CORDOVA.

A COMBINATION GRILLE AND BALCONY ON A HOUSE IN SEGOVIA.

A WROUGHT IRON WINDOW GRILLE IN SITGES, SPAIN

Roofs – Towers – Cornices

Minarets in the city of Tunis, Tunisia.

TILE ROOFED TOWERS IN ATHENS.

BRICK CORNICE IN ATHENS, AND AN OLD MOORISH HOUSE IN RONDA.

DETAIL OF AN OLD FARMHOUSE NEAR THE BAY OF ALGECIRAS.

A PROJECTING WOOD CORNICE ON A BUILDING IN SEVILLE.

DETAIL OF ROOF TYPICAL OF SOUTHERN SPAIN AND ROOF ON A BUILDING IN RONDA.

TYPICAL ROOF AND CORNICE TREATMENTS IN GRANADA.

CORNICE DETAIL ON A BUILDING OF THE GENERALIFE.

DETAIL OF THE GATE LODGE, ENTRANCE TO GENERALIFE.

TILE WINDOW AND DOOR HOODS, BUILDING IN SEVILLE.

TOWER ON A BUILDING ADJOINING EL GRECO HOUSE IN TOLEDO.

AN OLD COUNTRY HOUSE NEAR BARCELONA AND AN ELABORATE BRICK CORNICE, ZARAGOZA.

Courts and Patios

Oriental patio in a palace, Algiers.

Courts and Patios 111

IN THE CLOISTER OF THE OLD CAPUCHIN MONASTERY, AMALFI.

112   Courts and Patios

AN INTERESTING OLD COURT, SORRENTO.

TWO COURTYARDS, SYRACUSE.

PATIO IN THE HOTEL MADRID, SEVILLE.

A PLEASING ARCHITECTURAL TREATMENT OF A PATIO, CORDOVA.

TWO CHARMING PATIOS, CORDOVA.

A DELIGHTFUL OLD PATIO, CORDOVA.

COURT IN A HISTORIC OLD INN, TOLEDO.

COURTYARD OF AN OLD INN, TOLEDO.

Courts and Patios 119

IN THE GARDEN OF EL GRECO HOUSE, TOLEDO.

Garden Details

A PERGOLA TREATMENT OF A HILLSIDE, CAPRI.
INTERESTING USE OF TERRA COTTA JARS, CAPRI.

IN AN OLD GARDEN NEAR THE SITE OF ANCIENT CARTHAGE,
WALL FOUNTAIN AND POOL IN A GARDEN, RONDA.

OIL JAR USED AS A GARDEN FEATURE, ALGECIRAS, AND A WELL IN A GARDEN, ALGECIRAS.

LOGGIA IN A GARDEN, RONDA.

WALL FOUNTAIN IN THE GARDEN OF THE ORIENTAL HOTEL, ALGECIRAS, AND A WELL IN A GARDEN, ALGECIRAS.

POLYCHROME TILE SEAT IN A GARDEN, RONDA

ALABASTER FOUNTAIN IN A GARDEN, RONDA

DETAIL OF TILE SEAT, ALCAZAR GARDENS, SEVILLE.

128   Garden Details

FOUNTAINS IN THE GARDENS OF THE ALCAZAR, SEVILLE.

MORE FOUNTAINS IN THE GARDENS OF THE ALCAZAR, SEVILLE.

AN OLD MOORISH FOUNTAIN BOWL IN ALHAMBRA AND A GATE NEAR THE ALHAMBRA.

FOUNTAIN IN A PATIO, A HOUSE IN BARCELONA.

MISCELLANEOUS

POLYCHROME TILE DECORATING A GARDEN WALL, ALGIERS.

AN INTERESTING PROJECTING BAY ON A HOUSE IN TUNIS.

THE "NEW BRIDGE" AND BUILDINGS IN RONDA.

AN UNUSUAL PEBBLE AND COLORED TILE WALK, RONDA.

136 Miscellaneous

WROUGHT IRON JAR HOLDER, SEVILLE.

LAYING A PAVEMENT OF RIVER PEBBLES IN CORDOVA.

TERRA COTTA JAR AND WROUGHT IRON HOLDER, TOLEDO.

LANTERN IN THE GARDEN OF EL GRECO HOUSE, TOLEDO.

140 Miscellaneous

A PANELED AND DECORATED CEILING, BARCELONA.

DECORATIVE VALENCIA TILE IN A COURT, BARCELONA.

INTERIOR OF AN ARTIST'S COTTAGE, SITGES.

FIREPLACE IN ARTIST'S COTTAGE, SITGES.

Bibliography

Jackson, Parker H., "The Persian Water Rug Fountain: Balboa Park's Lost Treasure," *The Journal of San Diego History*, no. 4 (2000), <http://www.sandiegohistory.org/journal/200-4/fountain.html> (February 18, 2005).

Jackson, Parker H., "Richard S. Requa," *San Diego Biographies*, <http://www.sandiegohistory.org/bio/requa/requa.html> (February 18, 2005).

Jarmusch, Ann, "Requa revisited," 7 Sept. 1997, <http://www.signonsandiego.com/news/features/design/requarevisited.html> (February 18, 2005).

Schibanoff, James. M., "Requa & Jackson House in Peril," *Reflections*, no. 4 (2004), <http://sohosandiego.org/reflections/2004-4/batchelder.html> (February 18, 2005).

Showley, Roger M., "Requa's vision saved Balboa Park buildings," 14 Sept. 1997, <http://www.signonsandiego.com/news/features/design/requasvision.html> (February 18, 2005).